THE JEWISH NEW YEAR

A Crowell Holiday Book

THE JEWISH NEW YEAR

by MOLLY CONE

illustrated by JEROME SNYDER

THOMAS Y. CROWELL COMPANY

New York

CROWELL HOLIDAY BOOKS

Edited by Susan Bartlett Weber

Lincoln's Birthday	*The Jewish New Year*
St. Valentine's Day	*Columbus Day*
Passover	*United Nations Day*
Arbor Day	*Halloween*
Mother's Day	*Thanksgiving Day*
Flag Day	*Human Rights Day*
The Fourth of July	*Hanukkah*
Labor Day	*The Jewish Sabbath*

1 2 3 4 5 6 7 8 9 10

THE JEWISH NEW YEAR

Many moons ago, the blowing of a horn told the Jewish people of the new year.

It was not an ordinary horn. It was a shofar, the horn of a ram. And its sound was like no other. Perhaps that is why it was used to tell of things to come.

The horn blew loud at every new moon, but the blowing was loudest of all at the coming of the seventh new moon. This was a special time on the ancient Hebrew calendar.

For it was the season of the harvest. The figs were sweet. The apples were ripe, and the grapes deep purple. It was the end of the growing year. Time to begin again.

Today Jewish people still celebrate that beginning. They count it by the same ancient calendar. They even hail it with loud blasts on the same kind of horn.

It may be only the middle of September by today's calendar. But to Jews everywhere, it is the New Year.

The Hebrew calendar is very old. On it, the counting of the years starts with the time of the beginning of the world in the Bible.

The counting of the months begins in the spring. With the rise of each new moon, a new month begins. The seventh month is the holy month of the year, just as the seventh day is the holy day of the week.

The first ten days of the seventh month are set aside to celebrate each new year. The first day is called Rosh Hashonah. In the Hebrew language, these words mean the same as *beginning of the year*.

The tenth day is called Yom Kippur. It means *day of atonement,* or day for righting wrongs.

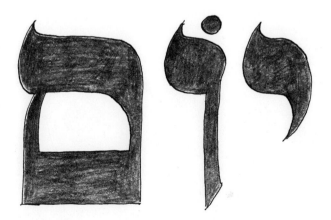

The ten days all together are known as Days of Awe. Rosh Hashonah and Yom Kippur are called High Holy Days, or High Holidays, because they are so important.

The world itself must have begun on Rosh Hashonah, Jewish people say. That was the time the new moon first rose on the new earth. The fresh waters came. The sun shone. Life began.

The Jewish New Year is always started with something sweet. It is a favorite beginning. On the first day children dip apple slices into honey. As they eat they wish, "May it be a good, *sweet* year."

Sometimes a whole fish is baked and served for dinner on the first night of Rosh Hashonah. The head of the family is served the head of the fish. But everyone wants to eat some of it and say, "May I be a *head* and not a *tail*." Everyone wants to be a leader in the coming year. Every child, of course, is hoping he will be head of his class.

In some families, carrots are served at Rosh Hashonah. "May we multiply," all say and giggle at the joke. *Carrot* and *multiply* sound the same in Yiddish, a language many Jewish people speak.

Usually there is some new fruit on the table. It is tasted for the first time at this holiday. Often it will be grapes, for grapes are gathered in the fall.

But the new fruit is not eaten until a special blessing is said. It is a thanksgiving prayer for all the good things that come out of the earth.

Many Jewish people have almost forgotten that Rosh Hashonah began as a harvest festival. Today the blessing of the fruit is the only reminder.

The counting up of the harvest became a time for another kind of counting up, too. On Rosh Hashonah, a legend says, the piercing sound of the ram's horn carries all the way to the ears of God. It reminds Him it is time to open the Book of Life.

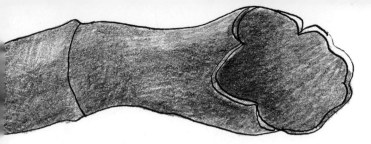

It is said that everyone's name is set down in the Book of Life. And under each person's name are listed his good and bad deeds. Once a year, on Rosh Hashonah, God opens the Book and counts them up.

On Yom Kippur, the legend says, God sets down in the same book each man's fate for the next year.

"How many shall die and how many shall be born . . . who shall become poor and who shall become rich . . . ." A person's fate is sealed on Yom Kippur, it is said.

On the days between Rosh Hashonah and Yom Kippur, a person has a last chance to look at his deeds. He can right his wrongs before his fate is sealed for the next year.

It is the custom for people to shake hands on Rosh Hashonah. They smile and say:

"May you be inscribed for a good year in the Book of Life."

The Book of Life is sung about in Psalms in the Bible. Other old writings tell the story of such a book, too.

Everyone must look back at himself is what the legend really says. Each one must judge his deeds as though God Himself were keeping count. To the Jewish people, Rosh Hashonah and Yom Kippur are the most solemn holidays of the year. They are days of prayer.

Perhaps the oldest New Year's custom of all is the blowing of the ram's horn, or shofar.

The ram was the animal Abraham sacrificed to God in place of his son Isaac in the story in the Bible.

The shofar is the same kind of horn Moses used to call his people to hear the Ten Commandments. The Bible says: "The voice of the horn grew louder and louder."

It is the same kind of horn Joshua and his people blew at Jericho. The Bible tells how the old wall shook with the noise. "At the sound of the horn, they let out a great shout and the wall fell down!" And they all marched in.

The shofar is not an easy horn to blow. What comes out sounds something like— T'KEE-OH! Or sometimes—T'RUUU-AH!

In ancient times, the shepherds called and answered each other across the hills with their shofars. Most often, the horn was blown to tell people when to stop work for the Sabbath. Sometimes it became a signal of alarm.

Now the sound of the shofar is heard only at the new year in most synagogues and temples. It is blown three times during Rosh Hashonah. And one long blast ends the prayers on Yom Kippur.

Hundreds of years ago, on the afternoon of Rosh Hashonah, everyone went to the banks of a stream. They turned their pockets inside out over the water.

It was a Rosh Hashonah custom to shake all sins into the water. Then the river would wash them clean, or carry them away.

To this day, some Jews still follow this old ceremony. They shake out their pockets and read prayers to say they are sorry for the mistakes they have made during the year.

A thousand years ago, and more, many people believed that bad luck could be given away. It was the custom to give it to a hen or a rooster on the day before Yom Kippur.

The hen was held by its feet. Then it was swung in circles over the head of the person who wanted to get rid of his bad luck. It was believed that all the bad would move from the person to the hen.

The hen was then killed—and the bad luck with it! After that, the hen was given to the poor for a good dinner.

Only one part of this old ceremony remains. It is a custom today to give something to the poor on the day before Yom Kippur.

Erev Yom Kippur, *the day before,* is almost as important as Yom Kippur day itself. It is the last day to mend quarrels. It is the last chance to correct mistakes. It is the day to forgive others, and to ask forgiveness.

No one knows exactly how this custom started. But it is a very important part of Yom Kippur.

First, people try to make things right with each other. Then they are ready to make things right with God.

Yom Kippur is a day of fasting. To eat nothing at all on this day is another ancient custom. It is as old as the blowing of the shofar. And it can be traced back to the Book of Leviticus in the Bible. "For on this day shall atonement be made . . . ."

Today, everyone except young children goes hungry all day long on Yom Kippur. In hunger, everyone suffers a little for all others who have ever suffered. Like the sound of the shofar, fasting on Yom Kippur touches the heart.

In most synagogues and temples, Yom Kippur begins with a song. It is the song of Kol Nidre. *Kol Nidre* are Hebrew words meaning *all vows* or *promises*.

No one really knows where this song came from, or who wrote it. The words were written down first. They are at least a thousand years old. The music was added hundreds of years later.

For a long time, Kol Nidre was not even part of the Yom Kippur prayers. But it came to have a special meaning for that day.

Some think the custom may have started with the Jews who lived in Spain five hundred years ago. Under a cruel ruler, they were not allowed to go on being Jews. They had to promise to give up their religion. If they did not promise they were killed.

Though they promised, many kept the Sabbath anyway. They prayed in secret. And on Yom Kippur they sang Kol Nidre. The words asked God to forgive them for making promises that had to be broken.

The Kol Nidre melody was very sad. Life for Jewish people was sad then too. But the music was also beautiful. Today the melody, not the words, is the important part. Some people call Yom Kippur evening "The Eve of Kol Nidre."

Long ago everyone wore special white clothes on Rosh Hashonah and Yom Kippur.

People dress up today, too. They wear their best to their synagogues and temples on the High Holidays.

To celebrate the New Year, the Jewish people blow a very old horn, pray and fast in a very old way, and sing a very old song. But they celebrate what never grows old. They celebrate hopes.

There are many hopes. But there is one hope that is stronger than all the others. It comes thundering out of the years like a shofar call.

"May it be Thy will, O Lord, to grant a good year!"

This wish is a wish that is always new. It is a prayer for all people.

The Jewish New Year is a holiday of hope. A time for remembering. A time for counting up. A time for righting wrongs. And a time to start all over again.

ABOUT THE AUTHOR

Molly Cone has written numerous books for boys and girls of all ages. She brings to the writing of *The Jewish New Year* a deep interest in Jewish lore and a gift for clear storytelling.

Mrs. Cone has been writing since she was a student at the University of Washington. She and her husband and children make their home in Seattle where they enjoy an active Northwest life.

ABOUT THE ILLUSTRATOR

Jerome Snyder, a native New Yorker, received his art training in New York City and in Europe. He has taught at Parsons School of Design, Cooper Union, and the American University in Biarritz, France. He is the recipient of a number of awards, including the Society of Illustrators Award of Special Merit. His works have been exhibited in the Museum of Modern Art, the Metropolitan Museum of Art, The Corcoran Gallery of Art in Washington, D. C., and in many other major museums; his illustrations have appeared in numerous magazines.

During World War II, Mr. Snyder served in the European Theater. He is now art director for a scientific magazine and lives in New York City.